Seduction Instruction for the Physically
Nonstandard Woman

by

Edward J. Harshman

Therefore, I hereby make a formal disclosure that I claim no verified expertise in the field about which I write, calling upon you the reader to decide on the value of the material on its own merits, meanwhile disregarding anything in my background that may suggest otherwise.

Preface, June 2017

In August 1995, I was swimming in the ocean, hit my head on the ocean bottom, broke my neck, and was paralyzed face down in the water for what seemed like a lifetime and very nearly was. Fortunately, a competent lifeguard rescued me and stabilized my neck. For about two months, my arms did not work right and I was not sure they ever would. (They do now, fortunately). Fortuitously, I had attended a conference about alternative human-interaction patterns in the context of men seeking women shortly before my injury. During my convalescence, living with my parents with limited-function hands and no access to research facilities or the medical or psychiatric community, I wrote this book and one other. The other got published easily; this one did not get published at all.

In July 1997, I entered a residency in physical medicine and rehabilitation, for doctors-in-training. I was disheartened to learn that organized medicine provided no help whatever in the form of psychological tactics and instruction to assist disabled or disfigured people to enter the competitive male-female marketplace and seek a mate. Personal self-affirmation, however helpful in helping someone recover from rejections, does not prevent rejections. I wanted something better, something that would help convert a probable rejection into being accepted so that a good relationship could start.

The Maine medical board tells me to get assistance from professionals with appropriate expertise if I publish anything. I can't unless such professionals exist.

There is no formal track record I can offer in support of this material. I can point to only one incident, which relies on an important theme in this book, that of reinterpreting a disability or physical liability as an asset and contriving to have a man agree that it is an asset too. In this incident, a young female patient who had Medicaid said she was considering breast enlargement because she felt unattractive to men. Aware that the cost of such surgery is not covered by Medicaid and is high, I suggested that she practice using her pectoral muscles to move her breasts seductively and noted that a large-breasted woman could not do so. She thereby would have that advantage, which could override the so-called disadvantage that her breasts were small. She seemed pleased. I, meanwhile, got the first test of my theory of having someone learn how to convert an apparent physical liability into, in the opinion of someone else, an apparent physical asset. The theory passed the test.

A link to an online copy of an earlier edition (unpublished) of this book was sent anonymously to the director of a summer camp, with an admonition to consider keeping me away from children. During my divorce, when conferring with the court-appointed guardian *ad litem*, I saw on her desk a paper copy of that same edition. My divorce is now final, and my ex-wife can no longer interfere with my intellectual property or my distribution of it. I want to help the disadvantaged: here, the disabled and disfigured women who are alone and not by choice. There is too much despair among such people. The medical board can tell me not to misrepresent myself, but it cannot tell me not to disseminate material at all. I will remain silent no more.

What follows was written by me in 1995, while my hands had poor coordination due to spinal-cord damage in my neck; and they ached while I typed. Nothing I learned during my residency suggested any changes to its content.

For this edition, I have made a bare minimum of changes, replacing mentions of cassette tapes with those of MP3 players, for example. Aware that my attitude toward women is now embittered due to a recent difficult divorce, I know that any alterations to the material are likely to undermine the theme and spirit of this book. Physically damaged women deserve no hostility from me; I have had to minimize recent editing to avoid allowing my current mindset to weaken or detract from what I had to say when I wrote it. The intent was to make something that is easy to read and is encouraging. It still is. Despite my current anti-female mindset, I hope I have succeeded to assist women exactly as I did when I wrote this book in 1995.

Edward Harshman

Seduction Instruction for the Physically Nonstandard Woman

October, 1995

Grief, recovery, and why this book is necessary

This book is for women with a physical handicap or disfigurement. Perhaps you had a serious injury that left you permanently scarred. Or major surgery, as for breast cancer. Or a neurologic loss, perhaps because of a stroke or a spinal-cord injury. So you need to adjust to your new body.

Or you could instead be a young woman, who never had a bad accident happen to her, but who just happened to have been born with a body different from that of other girls. Now, as you are approaching womanhood, you look at your body differently. Before, when playing with friends, being different wasn't very important after a while. After all, you got practice with making friends and having fun with them. But as a young woman, you have a new reason to look at your body differently. Most young women look critically at themselves when they hope to be attractive to young men. What used to be an ordinary part of your life has suddenly become newly important.

However it happened, you are physically different from most other people. If the difference is a bad one, then expect to feel upset as you think about it that way.

Losing something of value is a serious event. The expectation that you can interact with men the way other women do is important, and its loss is real too. Being very upset is normal. Misguided friends or counselors may try to console you by saying that the loss isn't very important. Or they may even keep you drugged, hoping to minimize your pain. Avoiding pain is good, usually; but shielding you from real feelings will slow down your adjustment. If you rely on someone else's belief that something isn't very important, then your feelings will get distorted. That means you won't be able to form relationships that are based on genuine feelings. To form a genuine relationship, you cannot dodge reality. If your loss feels big, then it is big. If it makes you cry, cry. Grieving, the process of adjusting to a major loss, is intense but temporary. Do not expect to be greatly distressed indefinitely, for there are new approaches to sexual attractiveness that you can learn. While you are recovering, a good psychiatrist can cautiously prescribe neuroleptics for you that can reduce your despair without significantly slowing your adjustment to your new body. But mood-altering drugs, if carelessly used, will slow or stop it. They can give you potentially permanent drug dependence. You will feel bad whatever happens; do not acquire a second problem,

Friends and others may be very concerned about you and offer compassion and help. That is generally a good thing, but it can establish bad habits. Becoming dependent on concerned friends is easy if they offer to things for you that you can do for yourself. It's not their fault; they're just trying to help you. And it isn't yours, either; for their offers can be genuine and can truly make you feel better. But just as a paraplegic in a wheelchair can become strong enough to wheel himself around and even climb curbs, you can become strong enough to seek and form relationships with men without depending on energetic friends or men who show interest in you only as a known act of mercy. Hard to imagine now, perhaps, but it can be done.

During your time of grief, you will feel unhappy whatever you do. Try to remain as independent as possible. Simplify your life, reducing your responsibilities by planning ahead. Try not to ask others for help. When you are feeling especially bad, avoid being seen or heard from except by close friends. Be perceived as self-reliant. If you truly can't do something that you want to, then pretend that you are doing it anyway, with your impediment magically solved. Doing so helps you keep a constructive attitude and will make further adjustment easy after the impediment is truly solved or otherwise reacted to. If you do not use your new handicap to get special consideration, then your grief will diminish after a month or two. Learn to function; do not worry about your attractiveness. That will come later.

The time when pure sadness becomes a frustration with not knowing how to continue with specific aspects of your life, but wanting to learn, is the worst time that you will ever have. It will get better.

When you can, however upset you remain, develop a clear wish for a sex life, and you are ready for further adjustment and personal change, then you are ready to proceed. Never mind how hopeless such a change may be, and forget everything you ever learned about how men insist that a woman have a perfect body. Pretend that you can make men attracted to you. Nice fantasy, right? Guess what? That fantasy can become reality.

Do not expect unconditional sympathy and cooperation as you try to improve your attitudes and your ego. Yes, handicapped people have a sex drive; but you already know that. Mainstream society merely permits it, without also supplying instruction. Modern politics includes identifying certain disadvantaged people as deserving special consideration, but without offering an effective way for such people to improve their lives so that they don't need special consideration any more. Black people are noted for being discriminated against, which is bad, and are herded into schools which teach black-dialect English so that no one will understand them when they graduate and they won't be able to get jobs. Dyslexic people, who have been told by schoolteachers that they have difficulty with reading, are often merely encouraged to develop and maintain good feelings about themselves; they might have been instead taught to read by the phonetic method instead of the politically popular whole-word method. Even AIDS victims, whose illness can often be cured, have been told that they have an incurable and fatal disease despite the brilliant and exhaustive research by Bryan Ellison that disproves its contagiousness and has, predictably, been viciously suppressed. The media seem more interested in eliciting feelings of compassion than in encouraging progress toward forever solving a problem. Because the material that follows can solve the problem of sexual unattractiveness, it removes a group of people from deserving a particular form of special consideration. Expect it to be considered politically incorrect.

If you have a nonstandard body and are unhappily unattached, then sooner or later you will wonder how to interact with men in a sexual context. Fortunately, new psychological techniques can be learned that have a good chance of creating a sexual relationship. They are likely to work with obesity, great age, terminal illnesses, or other disadvantages that are not generally considered true physical handicaps. They are less useful, unfortunately, when senses are impaired or there is a cognitive loss.

Details follow.

Introduction to the method

I present the method in three parts. First, develop confidence. Second, learn and practice specific skills. Third, assemble the skills into a seduction plan and apply it to the man or men of your choice.

Before doing anything else, get rid of some myths and misconceptions.

Myth: The process of interacting successfully with men will feel natural.

Reality: True, interacting with men naturally can feel natural. But interacting with men unnaturally, according to a planned pattern of seduction, may feel awkward. Be guided by what works. Not everything that is truthful, ethical, and of benefit to you will feel natural,

Myth: Attracting men is a combination of physical characteristics and inborn personality traits. It cannot be learned.

Reality: It can be taught and learned. I am trying to teach you.

Myth: A man's physical interest in an anatomically perfect woman is sealed into his permanent beliefs at an early age and is not changeable. Having a handicap, therefore, is a hopeless disadvantage.

Reality: Happily married people remain attracted to their spouses for many years, even though their appearance changes. And handicapped people of both genders can be attractive, however different they are from the media ideals.

Myth: Talking with and being polite to a man is enough. And if it isn't, then nothing can be done about it.

Reality: A man might otherwise be sexually interested in you, but not know how to say so because of your handicap. If a sensitive man does not know how to express his interest tactfully, then he may simply give up. To avoid losing opportunities, assume that a man considers your handicap a deterrent. If you do not take an explicit sexual initiative, then expect men to consider you a nice lady but nothing more. Ever. But if you take the sexual initiative, then he knows that it's possible and safe to express a sexual interest in you.

Myth: After you learn how to approach men sexually, other people who observe you will hope that you succeed.

Reality: Some acts are obviously allowed. Friendly greetings, nonsexual talk, and other safe activities are examples. Other acts are strongly discouraged. Seduction, or almost any other reference to sex or sexual activity, is neither. It may or may not be welcomed. Parts of our society discourage the solution of society's problems, as noted above. And some women will resent it strongly, as explained below. But if it works for you and harms no one, then the bad opinions of other people aren't very important.

Myth: There are many ways that women successfully use to make themselves attractive to men; and a woman can think carefully about which one or ones to use and, having done so, use them without further thought.

Reality: Seducing a man, like making a sandwich, is a multistep process. First you do one thing and achieve a result that isn't obviously useful. Then you use that result as the beginning of the next step to achieve a second result. Several results must be achieved in sequence. The mass media hope that you will think seduction takes only one step. They show you something you wish to do, perhaps being sexually attractive, and offer one product or one service and pretend that it will accomplish your wish in only one step. That way, you will buy it and not think that your wish is a problem any more. You already know that doesn't work.

Telling the truth, which is that seduction requires specific skills that you can learn but not have to spend money on, would ruin the media's marketing efforts. Clothing is an example of something you buy that you must, in general, wear continuously. And different clothes create different moods. But when you seduce a man, you must guide him through several states of mind. And while doing so, you cannot excuse yourself frequently and keep changing clothes as your man changes his exact mood. These facts disprove any implications that clothing should be worn to induce a precise state of mind. Clothing and cosmetics manufacturers have a reason to discourage disproof of this myth. I do not.

Myth: Nice ladies do not throw themselves at men.

Reality: If that is what is necessary to meet and seduce men, they do. And if the effort effects the wanted result, then they won't really mind making it. No rational man will be upset by receiving the attention of a nice lady. And other than the woman and the one man in whom she is interested, no one is directly affected.

Men, naturally, tend to prefer women who are clearly interested in them to women who aren't. That shouldn't be a surprise, for women prefer men who are obviously interested in them to men who are not. But there is pressure not to learn and react to this fact. A woman, handicapped or not, who is interested in men but doesn't show it is likely to resent women who do. A woman who doesn't show her interest in men would benefit if no one else did either, so that she would not be at a disadvantage. Seeing the problem, that other women let their interest show and she doesn't, she might decide to copy their ways and show her interest too. Then the competition would be more fair, and she and men would be happy. But instead, she often tries to censor the other women to match herself. She can use gossip, put-downs, and other pressuring tactics, hoping to discourage her successful rivals. Ironically, her acts can require more energy than doing things that work.

React critically to negative statements or gossip, especially if they contain emotionally charged language or lack facts. The myth has some truth, though. A nice lady does not openly throw herself at more than one man at a time. Men quickly learn that a woman who does so is generally a game-player and is best avoided. Also, nice ladies do not first call attention to themselves with an overtly sexual mannerism or statement. Women who do so tend to be game-players, too.

Myth: Men rarely receive sexual advances from women. Therefore, when they do, they will react with surprise and enthusiasm.

Reality: True, men rarely receive sexual advances from women. And when they do, they may react with enthusiasm. But a woman receives attention from men at least occasionally; and it is, to some extent, expected. When a man tries to start a conversation with her, she infers pretty quickly that he is interested in sex, or perhaps some other kind of relationship. A man receives such attention rarely or never. Do not expect him to infer instantly that you are interested in him. He may figure it out after you have given up on him and walked away, in which case both you and he will be frustrated. He is most likely to react with authority and enthusiasm if he is greatly experienced at meeting women. Otherwise, he may seem annoyingly reticent, seeming almost but not quite to turn you away. Be complimented by his inexperience, not discouraged by his self-restraint. He may be looking at you like the woman of his dreams, handicap and all, and wondering how not to lose you, meanwhile accidentally giving you a poor first impression. You will mean more to such a man, generally, than to an outspoken man who reacts confidently to you. Working with a shy man while totally confused about how he feels may be very trying. End your strain by spelling out your interest; make a date with him at once.

Myth: Nice ladies do not become physically intimate at first opportunity.

Reality: They do if they want to. But they don't accept just any man; they select the best possible man or men.

Myth: Nice ladies expect to be taken out, fussed over, and given gifts and other special treatment before permitting sex.

Reality: In an honest relationship, one that is not disguised prostitution (sex for material gain), a woman will give her man something, other than sex, that reciprocates for what she receives. The existence of romantic activity and gifts merely implies that the relationship is not purely sexual. It may include friendship or love, for example. Some truly nice ladies are slow to permit sex, and they enjoy receiving romantic treatment and give it too. But not all are.

Myth: A man who is otherwise suitable will lose interest if a woman permits sex too quickly.

Reality: He will lose interest if he cares only about playing the game, not about her. He will also lose interest if sex with her proves unpleasant (though it probably won't if you keep a creative and playful perspective, as I explain below). Either way, he is wrong for her. Screening out unsuitable men is quicker with prompt sex than with delayed sex. Having a relationship with an unsuitable man is using him. And the longer a bad relationship lasts, the worse you will hurt when it ends.

If you worry about losing a man's interest, be interesting. Display your personality, and make him keep your interest by displaying his. Give and receive sex as you wish, but try to offer and claim something other than sex too.

Myth: There is no reason to have sex as soon as possible, especially if the man and the woman are both willing to wait.

Reality: Seduction, though ideally enjoyable, is work. Your handicap adds to that work. It's exhausting to invest major effort in someone who will later prove uninterested. However friendly and eager he may seem in a nonsexual context, until you or he initiates sexual activity, you will not be certain that he will ever want it. He may say that he does, but you won't know his reaction to your handicap until you test him. To protect your effort and not waste it on an unsuitable man, confirm its effect as quickly as possible. Other women do not need to go through a special process like the one I describe below. You do, unfortunately. Defend your energy.

Myth: Desirable men can easily obtain the affections of able-bodied women. Less desirable men can't and must accept someone who isn't as attractive, namely, you. Therefore, the less desirable the man, the more likely he is to be interested in someone with a handicap.

Reality: The method that I describe requires that the man have good mental discipline and the ability to learn new concepts easily, i.e., intelligence. If a man isn't very bright, then he will probably be unable to understand as you talk to him according to my method; he will instead seem distracted and will make comments that follow from the general context instead of your exact words. Furthermore, desirable men have thought about what they want in a woman. Part of what makes them desirable is that there aren't important contradictions between what they look for and think they want and what they really do want. Because men are different from each other, they want different things in a woman. There is no single measuring system that every desirable man uses. Do not assume that you are second-best to someone else or that you are unattractive.

Myth: If a man cannot accept you as you are, even with your handicap, then he is not right for you. Therefore, you need only tell him about your handicap, clearly and without guilt, give complete and precise answers to his questions, and hope that he remains interested. If he doesn't, then there is nothing you could have done about it.

Reality: True, he will eventually need to know about and accept your handicap. But the more precise you get, the less sexually attractive you become—unless you encounter a man who is delighted to find someone with a handicap just like yours, which probably won't happen. As I will show, the most likely way to get a man to accept your handicap is not to tell him about it in detail as soon as possible. Instead, put him in a receptive mood and give him a vague description first. Specifics can wait.

Myth: Flirting, the playful exchange of attention with potential sex partners, is fun and does not involve any risk of being badly hurt by rejection. After all, a man can merely ignore a flirtatious act without offending anyone. Therefore, flirting is not only enjoyable but is also an ideal way to get to meet men.

Reality: True, flirting can be fun; and it is unlikely to result in painful rejection. But it permits role-playing and provides for a graceful rejection.

There are subtle differences between what is generally considered polite and what is most likely to work. You want the result: a man who is interested in you. It is occasionally necessary to do something that makes him feel awkward or which isn't as friendly as you might otherwise decide to do. The decision about flirting is one example. You don't want him to reject you. Therefore, you make rejecting you as difficult as possible.

To maximize your likelihood of establishing a relationship with someone, you will obviously be friendly and attractive, so that accepting your interest is easy and desirable. Less obviously, you will arrange your encounters with men so as to make rejecting your interest difficult and awkward. If a man is interested in you, great! But if he is not, then force him to say so outright. If you restrict his choice to cooperating with you or rejecting you awkwardly, then he may decide to cooperate with you briefly. You then have a chance of convincing him that you are worth knowing when you would otherwise have no chance at all.

A direct statement such as "Hi! I'd really like to meet you" is hard to turn down gracefully. Less direct statements, or nonverbal acts such as glances or winks, can be ignored or turned down easily. If you want the man's attention, then make it hard for him not to offer it.

Unfortunately, rejections from direct statements, when they occur, are more painful than are those from flirting. Being explicitly spurned can hurt. But by reducing the pain that may result from being rejected, direct statements can be made more desirable as serious seduction tools than is flirting. They work more often. Flirt just for fun or when you do not especially care about the outcome of doing so.

Learning how to represent yourself as sexually attractive is partly the acquisition of information and partly the development of new attitudes. If I give you only massive information, then you will not have to work with it and change your mindset. Conversely, with too little information you can develop a wonderful attitude but not have the facts to benefit fully from it, Therefore, I will give you basic principles and have you apply those principles to yourself in a way that works well for you. Ideally, you will derive information that helps you and, in doing so, think creatively and improve your confidence and attitude. You will note that everything I suggest that you think about will be enjoyable, not a dull drill or a recollection of painful memories. Change will not only be nearly painless but also, in its way, happy.

Let's get started.

Confidence-building 1: your competitive advantage

You are superior to other women in some very important ways. Learn them.

First, there is the strength that comes from adjusting to a disability or deformity.

If you have recovered from an injury or physical loss, or if you have lived with the knowledge that you are different from other girls, then you have survival skills unknown to most people. This is especially true if the loss or difference occurred during childhood, with its strong peer pressure. Unlike them, you know directly that life can go on for someone with a handicap. Except possibly in a social context, it can go on happily. In a social context, you may feel uneasy. But your perspective about life is probably sturdier than average, especially if your handicap is severe or if you were badly frightened by the injury that caused it.

Second, there is the relative freedom that you have merely because you are different.

Modern society contains many people without conspicuous handicaps and relatively few people like you. An important principle of social interaction is that the greater the number of people in a group or who are otherwise similar to each other, the more restricted the socially permitted range of conduct of those people. A sports hero or movie star, for example, may have eccentricities that would be condemned if found in someone who is not noteworthy. If your handicap is known, then no one will have a preconceived idea of how someone like you should behave. Therefore, society will permit conduct from you that it would shun if observed in others.

And the more options you have in a situation when dealing with people, the more power you have.

Because you are disabled, you are relatively powerful. Already.

It will be important to identify conduct that is permitted to you and to no one else. Almost no one will say to you, "This is OK for you and not OK for other people." But if you can learn it, then you can get away with some acts that would be otherwise frowned on or forbidden, including sexual initiatives. Access to such acts is an obvious advantage.

Beware compassionate people. Many of them are genuinely helpful. But some will try to do you favors hoping to offset your disability: "Let's be nice to her, because she's at a disadvantage." It's more pleasant when they're nice to you, but it's best if you really aren't at a disadvantage. And if you prove that you aren't, then those people might stop being so nice to you. So they're sort of bribing you to be relatively helpless. You're not. If they offer special favors that aren't unavoidably connected to a specific limitation, then you're probably better off declining.

Third, the human body adapts to specific handicaps with above-average development of its remaining abilities. A blind person, for example, is generally better able to hear and to infer from what is heard than is a sighted person. If you have lost the use of one hand, then after receiving rehabilitation you probably have unusual skill with your other hand. Wheelchair-dependent paraplegics and others often develop unusually strong arms.

Consider your handicap creatively, and try to identify what can be represented to others as a compensating strength. Make a list of favorable descriptions, ones that show your handicap from an advantageous perspective. Do not worry about strict scientific accuracy. Something that can be creatively presented and might be of interest to others is more useful than a clinical fact that has no intriguing possibilities. Favor descriptions that involve sexual activity or that include rubbing the skin.

After writing your list, read my list of possibilities and append from it to your list what you wish.

Paraplegia: wheelchair-dependent, arms strong, legs idle

Wrong: I cannot move my legs, so am trapped in a wheelchair.

Right: My arms are strong and skilled. I have had practice grabbing, jerking my hand, and letting go rapidly and in rhythm. This activity has been useful primarily to move about, but has other uses with the right man....

Hemiplegia: one-arm-drive wheelchair, either arm and leg strong, other arm and leg idle

Wrong: I can move about only in a special wheelchair, so am very limited.

Right: My one arm and leg are nearly useless; but who knows what I can do with my other arm and leg, or what wry facial expressions I can make when reacting to curious newsworthy events?

No pubic innervation: ordinary foreplay feels useless

Wrong: Sexual activity produces no pleasurable sensation, feels like a waste of time.

Right: In men, nerve pathways from the brain inhibit spontaneous erections. That's why doctors test lack of erections by looking for spontaneous erections at night, during sleep, when the brain does not inhibit them the same way as while awake. I wonder: is that nerve pathway missing in me, in which case I am more uninhibited than almost anyone? And some people with denervation like mine have an erogenous zone right above the level of denervation. Too bad self-stimulation does not work, so I cannot easily find it....

Brace-dependent: Must wear a device to function or to prevent injury

Wrong: I am disabled.

Right: I have a unique delicate aspect, yet am in some ways literally as strong as steel.

Mastectomy, one: One breast is missing; no reconstruction

Wrong: I look awful.

Right: How would I look in a swim suit that is patterned after a caveman costume, with an imitation-leopardskin fabric and one strap that goes over my one breast and its shoulder? And in an erotic performance like a striptease, one breast can be moved attractively much more effectively than can two in unison. By standing sideways, I can make the absence of the other one become scarcely noticeable.

Mastectomy, two: Both breasts are missing; no reconstruction

Wrong: I look awful.

Right: My ribs show very clearly. They have a ripply texture that few men have experienced; I can give them something new and wonderful if I wish.

Colostomy: Digestive products are released through a hole in your midriff, making you look odd.

Wrong: What a mess! I look awful.

Right: Digestive products no longer leave my body through the usual route, making it cleaner than in most people. If I do sit-ups with twists, alternately touching each elbow to the opposite knee, then I can strengthen my abdominal muscles and develop another coital site, with perfect voluntary muscular control over it, which will feel new and probably wonderful. (Check with your surgeon first; what I suggest may or may not be safe.)

Weakness in the lower cervical motor nerve roots (I had this affliction myself): The triceps muscles are weak.

Wrong: My arms don't work properly.

Right: I can pull you toward me, but I cannot push you away,

Age difference: You are interested in a man much younger than yourself.

Wrong: Relative to him, I am unattractive and feeble.

Right: I can offer him the wisdom of my experience and of my many years of practicing and perfecting lovemaking.

(Note: If you are middle-aged or older, then try to find friends and lovers who are much younger than yourself. If you confine social activity to people in your age range, then they are likely to become frail and unable to visit you just as you become frail and unable to visit them. Preventable loneliness results.)

Terminally ill, short life expectancy: Although not obviously handicapped, you have major cancer or another threat to life and do not expect to live long. Ethical considerations rule out seeking a multiyear relationship.

Wrong: What's the use? I will die soon anyway.

Right: I plan to make so much use of my next few months. I'm like a pixie: now you see me, now you don't.

Review that list carefully. It will improve your self-image.

Confidence-building 2: Make your own self-instruction audio track.

You now have a perspective of your handicap that represents it not as a disadvantage but, ideally, as a true asset. Next step: further improve your self-confidence by making a self-instruction audio track.

To derive material for it, write down at least 20 statements about yourself that describe you as powerful, confident, and socially skilled. You already have a few such statements that may need only minor revisions. Here is a list of criteria that the new statements are to follow:

1 Word them in the second person, as if someone is saying them to you.

2 Make them favorable statements, which you wish would be true if they are not already true. But they do not have to be really true.

3 They must have the potential to become true if they are not already true.

4 Don't let them compare you to anyone else or relate to factual standards of evaluation. But they may contain emotionally charged language, concepts, and opinions.

5 They may refer to actions, perceptions, or habits; don't let them assign you to existing categories by beginning "you are a" or "you will be a."

6 They may transform your handicap, or the process by which you acquired it, into a source of strength.

7 They may interpret any other distinctive characteristic of you, even if unrelated to your handicap, as an advantage.

Examples follow.

Good statement: "You can approach and talk confidently with an attractive man." It may not be true right now. But it has the possibility of becoming true.

Good statement: "After being badly frightened by the auto accident/gunfire/unanesthetized emergency surgery, you are not afraid of ordinary social putdowns." This statement converts your history into a source of strength. It can become true if it is not true already.

Good statement: "If it works, you will enjoy it. If not, you will learn from it. You cannot lose." This attitude makes social or seduction interaction into a blend of fun and learning. I particularly like this statement, for I would never have learned enough to write this book if I hadn't made a horrendous series of mistakes.

Good statement: "If you are interested in a man, then he is very lucky." This statement will become true as your skill and confidence increase. It obviously has the potential to become true.

Good statement: "You will not settle for the worst men; you will select the best men." If you can attract especially good men, then this statement will be true. If not, then you can make it true by learning how to do so.

Good statement: "Men will find you irresistibly attractive." This statement may become true, however improbable it may appear right now.

Bad statement: "You can seduce any man you want." However desirable such an ability may be, it is unrealistic. Some men are homosexual, happily married, or just plain not interested whatever you do.

Bad statement: "Your handicap will not be noticed." It will be. I will show you how to have it perceived as an asset, however, so that it will not needlessly interfere with you in a seduction context.

Bad statement: "You will become more skilled than Miss Other Woman." Potentially true or not, a statement that measures your skill and success by comparing you to someone else is not very useful. Of ultimate importance is your meeting and seducing good men, however successful another woman is or becomes at doing so. Do not let someone else divert your energy.

Bad statement: "You are a wonderful person." A "You are a" statement, however favorable, is likely to generate internal "no, I'm not" resistance.

Bad statement: "I can meet four new men daily and not get upset if nothing works out with any of them." A happy statement if true, and a worthwhile target if not yet true. But the quota gives it too much precision. This precision will feel pressuring and not encouraging. If you think of quotas as a useful motivating force, then set and use them. But not on the audio track.

To think of additional statements, consider someone who is confident and whom you admire. Favorable statements about this person may be potentially true about you. If you can write down 20 or more statements (the more, the better), do so. If not, keep trying. Think of your favorite people and their skills and attitudes; they will give you ideas. If stuck, set your incomplete list aside and try to add more statements the next day. Do not expect to think of all 20 statements at once.

Having completed your list, read it into a high-fidelity audio recorder, perhaps a computer, perhaps a smartphone. Portable devices can introduce substantial background noise or have a low-quality microphone; connect an external microphone to a separate recording device if possible. Read with authority and confidence; your tone of voice will be critical. Forcing an authoritative tone and retaining it for the necessary five minutes or so may be very difficult; pretending you are talking to a friend may help. Keep trying until you get a good authoritative-sounding error-free audio track.

You now have a five-minute self-instruction audio track. Because it exactly matches what you want to become, it is likely to work better for you than can commercially available products. And the process of making the audio track forced you to think and fantasize, in fun and constructive ways, about your future. Did reading the statements authoritatively feel odd or alienating? Yes? That just means that your self-image is unfavorable—for now.

For a second audio track, record a brief introduction such as "Hello, (your name). You are about to grow strong and develop new self-confidence." Then, create a third audio track that consists of the content of the second one followed by a few hours that comprise numerous copies of the first audio track. Finally, record a conclusion such as "These new skills and attitudes will infiltrate you and make you grow strong. Good night."

This third and last audio track, the final product, contains an individually created self-instruction speech. Play it every night as you fall asleep. Your familiar voice will implant new and constructive attitudes in you while you cannot consciously resist. Because you made your own audio track, the attitudes will exactly match your needs.

Expect to feel temporarily uneasy in social situations after about a week, but permanently confident in them after about a month. As your attitudes improve, you may want to change the statements and make another audio track. But ideally, you will not need to use an audio track for very long.

Confidence-building 3: he wants you until proven otherwise

If you see a man and are interested in him, in that you would be happy if he tried to start a conversation with you and considered a relationship of some kind, then he may or may not be or become interested in you. If you are interested in him, then there are four possibilities:

1 You act as if he is interested in you, and he is interested in you. This possibility is the happiest for everyone; a relationship can form.

2 You act as if he is interested in you, and he is not interested. His reaction may be a sympathetic rejection, or it may be less pleasant. Not good, but the incident is short-lasting and survivable.

3 You ignore his potential interest, and he is interested in you. Too bad; you threw away a possible relationship.

4 You ignore his potential interest, and he wasn't interested anyway. Nothing happened.

Obviously, you will want to maximize the likelihood of possibility 1. If you ignore a man's potential interest, then you risk losing a relationship as in 3. Unfortunately, if you assume that a man is interested, then you will risk 2. But if the unhappy feeling that results from being rejected can be reduced or eliminated, then you will not mind that possibility— and you will have access to interested men that you would otherwise not know about. By raising the likelihood of risk 2, you reduce or eliminate risk 3.

What I propose, therefore, is an exchange of one problem for another. If you can somehow not care about being rejected (2 won't bother you), then it will be easy for you to reach out to men and meet them easily and often. If. That will take some work. But it can be done.

But there is another fact. You can create interest if a man does not already have it. Doing so reduces risk 2 still further, for it won't be as likely to occur.

Unfortunately, you cannot expect men to react happily to your mere presence. A known handicap makes men believe that they risk accidentally offending you. And if they don't want to offend you, then they are motivated to stay away. So you must compensate by taking the initiative yourself. But you can. You have a wider range of socially permissible behavior than do most women, remember? You can get away with social aggression when and where most women cannot. Gather strength from that fact.

Make the first move.

Approaching men sexually may seem frightening and unnatural. But that's not what matters. If what's natural doesn't work, do something unnatural instead. Martial arts experts know this fact, and they are very good at unnatural but effective self-defense tactics. Being effective is a higher priority than being natural.

Being rejected is always a possibility. But hostile rejections are relatively rare. Most include some gratitude for trying and an attempt to make you not regret having done so. Are you afraid of being nastily rejected, so that you feel hurt and without an appropriate reaction for being treated poorly? That risk can be reduced greatly by simply forming a new mental strategy. Are you afraid of encountering total despair if turned away? That risk can be eliminated completely, as I will show.

Remember: until proven otherwise, he wants you. Just go over and take him.

Confidence-building 4: Elicit and recall a confident mood.

Social situations for any handicapped person can be awkward. But not all situations are social. Think of a context in which you felt confident. (Remembering a real one is ideal. But imagine one if you cannot remember a real one.) The context need not involve other people. Perhaps it is one in which you are repairing a computer. Or cleaning a floor. Or driving to an unfamiliar destination without getting lost. Or even doing exercises to get your body into the best condition possible. When you have identified a context, visualize it, recall its sounds, and note how confident you feel.

So far, you have not begun to apply this confident feeling to social situations, including meeting men. Right now, it is more important to experience this feeling than to worry about applying it. Close your eyes, think, recall, imagine, and fantasize until the confidence gets really strong.

Then, stop. You are unquestionably in a mood that would be useful in a social situation if only you could take it with you. You can. Here's how:

Recall Pavlov's experiment with a dog and a bell. After the dog learned to expect food when the bell was rung, the dog reacted to the sound of the bell by salivating. A link was established between the sound and the food; salivating proved that the link existed.

Your feeling of confidence is something that you want to induce. Not by actually ringing a bell, of course. Instead, you want to link it to some event, so that when the event occurs you enter the confident state. Choose an event that you can control perfectly. Pinching yourself in a certain place is a possibility; I will use it as an example. Close your eyes and restore that confident feeling. When it is really strong, pinch yourself. Repeat that exercise once or twice a day, and do not pinch yourself in that place except when doing the exercise or, later, when the link is established, you want to feel really confident. When the link is established, you will be able to induce self-confidence by pinching yourself if you do not do so too often.

Re-enter that confident state. (Enter it as often as you wish, and retain it for as long as you want. If it becomes a major component of your personality, then you have been helped and not hurt. Do not fear dependence on good things.) A confident feeling is a desirable and happy condition as such, without being studied in detail. But analyzing it is useful; it has a subtle component that is very important.

Life is not perfect. Because you are handicapped, you are probably more aware of that fact than are most people. Small children learn to solve problems and overcome obstacles in various contexts, and they develop self-confidence in those contexts. Confidence requires not only an immediate feeling of happiness, but also a sense of the power to defend your happiness successfully against various minor or substantial threats. While in your confident state, imagine something going wrong. You immediately know how to react, either to correct it or to ignore it. You are in control.

From now on, when entering your confident state and creating the link to pinching yourself, note your ability to withstand minor setbacks or other unpleasant circumstances. You will want to recall that ability whenever you induce self-confidence, for it will make setbacks feel very unimportant and easily forgotten.

After the link is created, you can jump-start your confidence in a social situation by appropriately pinching yourself. Do so, when you need to.

Confidence-building 5: Your vicious-circle feedback loop

Yet another source of confidence can be developed. Perhaps you have had the misfortune of being with a man whose physical interest in you was not completely mutual. "Don't fight me off," he said; "that just makes me more eager." Whatever you did, resisting him or not, you felt trapped. Not good.

Now, imagine that he continued, saying in full, "Don't fight me off; that just makes me more eager. And if you turn me down, then I will merely take my fully aroused self away and go find another woman." Not very flattering, but at least he would take no for an answer.

Try to adopt his mindset.

Create a link in your mind between being turned away and going away not sadly, but with new energy. Imagine being turned away and enthusiastically replying, "Aha! I just learned something about how not to seduce men. Thank you very much for showing me. You'll never know what that lesson was. But I do. It will be very helpful. I can hardly wait to put it to use. Bye!" Close your eyes and remember a time when you were rejected. Remember in detail what you said and did, what you saw and heard, and what he said and did. Make it like watching a movie. Then change the script. Add a scene in which you say "Aha! Thanks for the lesson!" right after being turned away. Add as much detail as you can. Make him look at you sheepishly, as if he wondered what kind of wonderful person he was pushing away. And make yourself leave him with new energy and confidence. Remember another time when you were rejected. Remember it in detail, like a movie; and add a similar scene. Repeat for as many rejections as you can remember.

Forming the habit of reacting to rejections with new energy will encourage you to keep trying when rejected. This habit resembles a vicious circle: rejection then energy then rejection then energy, etc. Sooner or later, you will not be rejected. This analysis, of course, assumes the worst possible premise: many consecutive rejections. Either you get more and more energy, or a nice man is quickly found who accepts you. Both outcomes are desirable.

Try not to make movie-rewrites of imaginary rejection scenes, those in which you might meet a man but have not actually done so. Do not mentally practice getting rejected. If you want to imagine scenes in which you meet someone, then make them happy ones in which everything works out. They will help you feel good about yourself, and they're fun anyway. Direct most of your mental energy toward successful seduction, not toward damage control when seduction fails. Only the former outcome is a true net benefit.

Confidence-building 6: Forewarned against putdowns is forearmed.

Approaching a man, if you realistically fear being turned away rudely (because of your handicap or for any other reason), can be an unnerving concept. Having to allow for a rude response is, alas, reasonable. Being hurt by it, however, can be made unlikely—and not just by internal rationalizations about how bad a particular man proved to be.

Consider this scenario: You make a friendly remark to a man, trying to start a conversation. He ignores you or says something nasty. You feel hurt and angry, and you don't know what to say or do in response. Most therapists would suggest that you accept the pain, recover from it, make some rationalization that it was his loss and not yours, and try to forget it. I do not agree; the incident not only can be linked to a lesson-learning source of strength, but also can be almost completely prevented. You need only to plan ahead.

Before approaching a man and speaking to him, you will have in mind something to say. You hope that he will respond civilly and that he will be nice to you. But you know that he might not be nice. If he is nasty, then having a witty rejoinder to his nastiness will keep you from feeling totally defeated. He verbally hits you; you verbally hit him back. Your self-respect remains. If you demonstrate superior wit, then he will be unable to reply to you without sounding ridiculous. Winning the verbal battle will increase your self-confidence, a very good outcome considering that the same incident might have damaged it instead.

Have some introductory statements ready. Pair them with retorts that you will use if, after using the introductory statements, you are insulted. Here are some examples; try to write your own. Even if you feel content with these, the act of writing other statement-retort pairs will help you think creatively and with authority. I highly recommend the mental exercise.

Statement: You look like someone I'd like to know / really handsome / open-minded / (anything positive).

Retort: Appearances can be deceiving.

Statement: Hello. May we talk for a while?

Retort: What an efficient statement! I wish I could say everything I know that simply.

Statement: I'd like to know someone like you.

Retort: Thanks. Now I know what a foul-mouth bigot is like.

Turn an obscene remark to your advantage. If you hear one that suggests a sex act, smile gently and say "Hmm. An interesting idea." Then, after a brief pause, announce decisively, "No, you're not my type." This response of yours accomplishes three things for you. First, you defend successfully against the verbal attack. Second, you represent yourself as attractive enough to pick and choose. Third, you leave witnesses wondering if they are your type, provoking sexual interest without having taken the risk of first mentioning sex. Expect nearby men to become at least mildly interested in you; exploit that interest by striking up a conversation.

Occasionally, you will be turned away rudely and will have no witty retort available. Consider such incidents as reminders to learn more, and you will never be caught twice by the same insult. The process of learning will not be perfect. Decide now, however, that you will protect yourself as well as possible and that you will repair any weaknesses in your verbal armor as soon as you discover them.

Do not use your retorts when you are turned away politely. Some men are happily married and will appreciate your attention, even though they will not accept offers of intimacy. If a man turns you down nicely, then remember that you have not been insulted or even hurt. You have merely received an unintended setback, delivered with as much kindness as possible. React accordingly, matching his tact with your own.

Next, learn some specific skills.

Seduction preparation 1: Learn about the profound question.

By now, you have learned six ways to boost your self-confidence and how and why to approach men. There is a transition, however, from being recognized as a human being to being perceived as an interested and desirable potential sex partner. Following only the earlier instructions is likely to induce many incidents in which a man looks at you and thinks, "She's a nice lady, and I sort of feel sorry for her. But a sex partner? No. She's just not for me." When you are talking with a man, you don't want his attention to wander freely to your handicap and make him decide against you. Instead, try to divert his attention from your handicap until you can have him perceive it as an asset. Seizing his attention and controlling it until you can change his opinion seems unrealistic. But although unnatural, it is fairly easy to do.

Before trying to learn how to divert attention, stop and answer this question: If you meet and marry the perfect man within the next year, then what will your bedroom look like five years from now?

I don't need to know your answer, of course. But you needed to experience the process of creating the answer. You had to think carefully, and you probably had thoughts or fantasies about the ideal husband and about your future home or community. While thinking, you ignored the facts that you were reading this book and that you have a handicap.

You now know that one carefully designed question can keep a man from thinking about your handicap. It can also induce a useful mood.

Lacking a formal name for such a question, I will call it a profound question.

Criteria for a profound question:

1 It is sufficiently obscure that it has probably never been asked, to the same person, before,

2 It sounds friendly. Most profound questions will seem too personal right after you meet someone; you will have to establish a mutual feeling of friendship before asking them. But you don't have to ask it immediately. Wait for, or create, the right context, and they will seem innocent.

3 It is somewhat hard to answer, requiring significant thought and analysis.

4 It can be answered only by imagining or otherwise thinking about facts and feelings in a different context from the actual setting that you and he are in. "How do you like the snow?" is easy to answer during a blizzard. But on a hot summer day, you have to think about cold and winter to answer it.

5 Answering it puts a person into a predictable state of mind, one that is to your advantage.

Careful use of profound questions can put men into useful moods. They are powerful tools, not only of seduction but also of other forms of interaction. Here is another example of a profound question, one that is convenient if you just saw a man and want him to take the initiative when talking with you.

"Excuse me, sir. What would I have to say to make you happy that I approached you?"

A reasonable answer to that question requires the man to consider the process of meeting women. It forces him to think, distracting him from your handicap. Finally, it has him tell you exactly what he wants to hear, which you promptly echo back to him. After a good laugh, you tell him,

"I'm so happy you noticed me."

You noticed him first, of course. But he may not remember that.

You promptly put him into a meeting-women state of mind. Not only that, but you also caused some confusion about who was trying to meet whom. You did that by first approaching him, then replying as if he approached you.

There is a discrepancy between what you said and what really happened. It seems obvious enough here, when you can study the dialog at your own pace; but it won't necessarily be to a man when you are actually approaching him. The discrepancy is likely to cause subconscious confusion.

Successful child psychologists know about subconscious confusion. A common example is the practice of giving an order to your child, then saying "OK?" The phrasing of the question seems to demand a yes or no answer. But the correct answer may be "I understand, but I disagree." The child can't figure out that the simple question deserves a complicated answer and gets confused.

Confused children are likely to misbehave. Adults who encounter such confusion usually, instead, react in whichever way is easiest. So you merely make sure that what is easiest is beneficial to you. But if the confusion doesn't have a subtle cause, then it won't be subconscious. It will be obvious. He may challenge therefore your words: "What did you mean by that?" You can't induce subconscious confusion without something that is subtle and fairly complicated.

Subconscious confusion is helpful to you. If a man feels it, then he will probably try to resolve it instantly even if the truth is slightly distorted in the process. Your final statement, therefore, has a good chance of making the man believe that he took the initiative. He may even follow through as if meeting you was his idea.

Incidentally, have a retort ready in case of a rude reply. Consider "If you can't think of anything either, then we're REALLY in trouble" to the question. Or later, if he protests when you refer to his noticing you, then say sweetly, "But you responded when I spoke. You did notice me."

Seduction preparation 2: Practice the three-year-old state of mind.

As shown below, my seduction method requires placing a man in a psychological state in which he thinks like a three-year-old boy. Yes, you can learn how. But you need some practice first.

Alone, away from prying eyes and ears, recall or imagine your life as a three-year-old girl. Practice reciting your memories and fantasies. Mention real or fictitious adventures of a younger sister or childhood friend, if you wish. Prepare separate narratives, at least one that has each of sight, sound, and touch as the most important sensation. Recite them several times in advance. Out loud. (Go ahead; no one will hear you.) Be able to tell them to a man whom you have recently met.

Seduction preparation 3: Practice describing your handicap in a sexual tone and context.

First, design an appropriate description of your handicap. Second, practice reciting it in a sexy voice. Out loud again. Precise facts about your handicap sound clinical and impersonal, and they force attention to it instead of to you. Try instead to announce its immediate sensual consequences; feel free to be vague about its type and formal medical name. Doing so will make the man wonder what the handicap is (if it is concealed) or its exact characteristics (if visible). Stay vague. If he knows exactly what the handicap is, then he can stereotype you. Stereotypes are likely to prejudice him against sex and to be harmful to your cause.

Write and memorize a description of your handicap that, to the extent possible, follows these rules:

1 Refer to skin against skin or to the act of undressing or being undressed.

2 Encourage or require imagination or wondering, without telling all about your handicap and its consequences.

3 Represent your handicap as enjoyable in a sexual context and as a new adventure.

4 Make your handicap seem like an advantage—even if you have to use unusual criteria to do so.

Your reference may resemble one of your self-confidence statements that you developed and worked with earlier. But it will not necessarily be identical. Here are some examples; write your own if you want or need to do so.

Paraplegia: My arms are especially well-developed. (Move them slowly up and down, open palm facing him.) When I feel good about someone, I can hold him tightly. Very tightly.

Hemiplegia: I have had great instruction and practice with one arm and one leg. When I'm in bed, lying on my side, well ... you know how it is.... (He doesn't! You forced him to imagine you in bed and wonder what could happen.)

No pubic innervation: My sensitive areas are not so much here (point to your breasts and crotch—which calls attention to you in a sexual context) as right around where the nerve pathways fade away... I keep thinking how it would feel if someone held me just right.... (You made him wonder exactly how and where to hold you.)

Brace-dependent: This device makes me strong. I'll show you what I can do with it. Guess what I have hidden here.... (Some braces have unintended hiding places for condoms or other useful objects. Displaying a condom may feel excessively forward, but it will create a strong visual link between your brace and sex. If you think you can get away with showing a condom while smiling knowingly, try it.)

Mastectomy, one: The way I am built lets me do something most women cannot. (Good! You represented yourself as having an advantage.) How do you think I would look in a swim suit that is patterned after a caveman costume, with an imitation-leopardskin fabric and one strap that goes over my one breast and its shoulder? I've always wondered about that. (He will, too. Forget the indecent-exposure laws. You won't get arrested just for bringing up an image.)

Mastectomy, two: My ribs are visible. Very visible. (Rub your hands over your chest and sides.) They have a ripply feeling, sort of like a vibrator, if you rub them the right way. (Note the second-person reference: "you" rub them.... That is a subtle reference to his rubbing them, an idea that you want to encourage.)

Colostomy: When I get really close to someone, I can offer him physical intimacy with (hold up your hand with the thumb and second finger touching and slide the thumb and finger tips repeatedly past each other, making a circle that contracts and expands) perfect muscular control. (Point to the colostomy site.)

Obesity: My body is soft and snuggly, and if I crawl on top of you in an intimate context I can make you completely helpless.

Age difference: I have been alive for a great many years. I have experienced (list various unusual experiences). When I am really at ease with someone, my feelings come out ... so much to share ... so much

49

to show. (You have changed the criterion of attractiveness from appearance to wisdom, making yourself unusually desirable.)

Terminally ill, short life expectancy: When I think of compressing my life into just a few months, my feelings get so intense. Think of what would happen if you had only a day to live. (Believe it or not, the normal reaction to imagining such a short life expectancy includes dramatic sexual activity. Watch him and wait for a few seconds; make sure he is thinking about that before continuing.) Now you know what I'm thinking.

Having learned a suitable description of your handicap, practice reciting it properly. Use a suggestive voice; sigh or moan when appropriate. If you have difficulty using a sexy voice to describe your handicap, then record one or two suitable television advertisements that use woman models to sell clothing or cosmetics. (Audio only; don't bother with the video recorder.) Then play the recording, meanwhile reciting the words of the commercial and trying to sound like it. Repeat until you can match its tone exactly, and then start practicing the description of your handicap.

Be too melodramatic, not too restrained, if you must misjudge yourself. How your description is perceived by others is more important than how it sounds to you. People who have been restrained or repressed, as by a handicap and its consequences, tend to overestimate their nonverbal impact when they express feelings.

Seduction preparation 4: Learn sex technique and adapt it to your handicap.

Eventually, after seducing a man, you will not want the actual sex act to disappoint him. Prepare by reading sex-technique manuals and becoming familiar with what they teach. If certain techniques appear fun but you are too weak to use them because of a neurologic or other difficulty, then study others, do exercises until you are strong enough, or consider special arrangements of pillows, braces, straps, or anything else that may help. Ask your doctor or physical therapist about useful devices. (Don't be embarrassed. They may be very knowledgeable and be afraid of embarrassing *you* if they ask first.) If you are substantially paralyzed, then plan on being swung from a trapeze bar or other lifting device; do not expect to please someone greatly by merely lying passively. Think ahead. Be able to give a man the best time of his life. Because so few women study and practice sex techniques in advance, you will probably give him a wonderful experience that he will remember forever. Other women won't. You have yet another advantage over them.

Don't be embarrassed about borrowing or buying such books. People expect to lend or sell them; otherwise they would not be displayed in libraries or bookstores. React to unpleasant remarks with a gentle smile, so as to say "You'll never know what you're missing." Some people who watch you will be surprised, but not hostile. Let them watch you and learn.

The preparation is over. Let's do it!

Seduction step 1: Establish verbal contact.

Take the initiative. You will not be significantly bothered by putdowns.

Try to appear friendly, enthusiastic, and interested in only the man to whom you speak. If you make a halfhearted attempt at approaching a man, then a failure will be less upsetting than if you commit yourself fully to the attempt. But you will be more likely to fail. You already know that failing is not a serious matter. Maximize your chance of success, put all of your energy into the attempt, and be direct. Do not flirt.

Introduce yourself to the man of your choice, then lay claim to a few minutes of his time or make a date with him.

Seduction step 2: Drive the man into a three-year-old state of mind with a profound question.

As a boy, he learned what criteria to use when considering a woman's sexiness. And as a boy, he can re-learn them. In your favor, of course. So you will reverse the process by which his sex attraction criteria were earlier learned. He learned them at approximately three years of age. Put a man in a three-year-old state of mind, able to unlearn and relearn as does a three-year-old, and it won't be very difficult to teach him.

Is it ethical to tamper with a man's feelings so as to make him consider you attractive? Definitely. You are not going to deceive him or lie to him. Hair dye and suggestively padded clothing are considered fair by many women, even though they deliberately deceive. And you are not speaking ill of other women, making them appear bad or inferior. You are merely speaking well of yourself. You have a right to exist and to be perceived in the most favorable way that is truthful. If a man has not considered you from a flattering perspective that matches the facts perfectly, then you have a right to direct his attention and make him do so. You are different from most other women, and your methods will be different too. Do not consider them wrong just because they differ from those used by others.

Not everyone shares my ethical belief; some lawmakers disagree. Using these methods to induce sexual activity may or may not be legal. I dare not guarantee approval of these methods by law enforcement authorities, however much I wish to do so. Banning these methods, however, suggests that they work. And harassing a handicapped woman merely for living fully would be a politically disastrous act. Nevertheless, be warned.

After talking casually for a minute or two, ask the appropriate profound question, one that puts him into a three-year-old state and makes him associate it, and you, with enjoyment:

"It's so important to get fun out of life. How does your concept of fun differ now from what it was when you were twenty, ten, or even three years old?"

The question does not immediately query the man about his fun at age three. The transition would be too abrupt, making him uneasy. The question carefully seems to make three-year-old fun the end of a logical sequence instead of an apparently randomly chosen concept.

Expect the man to remember or imagine having fun as does a three-year-old. He may find these thoughts embarrassing, especially if he is a stodgy and dignified gentleman. To minimize his discomfort and encourage this state of mind, share your carefully rehearsed memories or fantasies of yourself as a little girl; sound spontaneous and giggle freely. Keep him talking.

While sharing these memories and fantasies, observe him carefully. Remember those three-year-old descriptions? Now's when to use them. Does he seem most interested in visual images? Then describe your child-like scenario in a visual way, emphasizing appearance. Does he seem most interested in sound? Then emphasize sounds, perhaps wind through trees or very quiet footsteps. Does he react most strongly to touch? Then emphasize skin-contact sensation.

Sound girlish and lighthearted; remember that you are trying to appear fun and uninhibited and not as if you are carefully planning to seduce anyone. Skillfully done, this process will get a man into a three-year-old state of mind.

Keep observing him. When you are sure he is in a boyish mood, direct the conversation to body contact between two people, perhaps friendly parent-child roughhousing. Children often cannot easily distinguish between pretending and reality; this concept is legitimately interesting and is a plausible introduction to a story in which someone's father is a dragon who carries you away, etc. Call attention to the feel of skin against skin.

Seduction step 3: Announce your handicap.

From child's play in which children handle each other, change the subject to differences between people. Children are small, grownups are big. Men have low voices, women have high voices. Parents give big hugs, little sisters give weak ones. He has (a characteristic of normal men, the opposite of your handicap), you have.... Now, it's time to tell him. Use your previously prepared and rehearsed description.

You just told a man about your handicap so as to induce sexual interest. Never again will you think that action impossible.

If he wants more information than you give him, then react exactly as if he was making a pass at you and you were really interested. Smile, sigh, squeeze his hand or embrace him, and suggest continuing the discussion in a private place. Do not end his suspense.

Seduction step 4: Make him retain his interest until you can act on it.

Unfortunately, you and he will probably be in a semipublic place where uninhibited sex is impractical. Protect yourself from having his interest fade.

First, remember Pavlov's dog and your link: pinching yourself brings self-confidence after you have trained yourself. Create a link in him. You have induced sexual interest; link it to reproducible stimuli that you can repeat later. While alluding to your handicap, give visual, auditory, and kinesthetic stimuli; for the simultaneous use of many senses creates a strong composite stimulus. Use a sexy voice (hearing). Tilt your head or use a subtle eye gesture (sight). Take him by the wrist, or use a special grip on his hand that no one else is likely to have used before (touch). Pause for about a second; let the stimuli receive an internal reaction. Then, talk about romantic or intimate feelings, pretending that a relationship already exists.

Second, drive your handicap, previously represented in a sexual context, into long-term memory. After about 20 minutes have passed from when you first mentioned it, bring it up again. The process of remembering is different if something has been remembered for longer than about that time. By making him recall it, you help him remember your attractiveness indefinitely instead of for only a few minutes. Bring it up politely, but explicitly enough that he has to respond.

An effective, though awkward-feeling, way to bring it up is to refer to it somewhat abruptly—then apologize for interrupting him or changing the subject. Apologize for forcing the idea on him, and suggest that he will be reminded of it from time to time: "Oh, dear. Now I got you thinking about my handicap (appropriate description) again. That's such a nuisance. The more you try to forget something, the more you have to think about it. (Fidget, pretending to be nervous.) And maybe you'll always think about it whenever you see me." You sound so regretful that he has no reason to complain. But you just linked his seeing you to his thinking of you as especially attractive, and you paradoxically made the link hard to forget by commenting on the act of trying to forget it.

Like any woman, you will protect yourself. Follow recommendations from your police department, and verify the man's identity and that he can be traced if necessary. Also, beware sadomasochists if you are disfigured; and be especially careful of rape if your mobility is impaired.

Seduction step 5: sex at last

At first opportunity, arrange for yourself to be alone with him. Repeat the three-sense stimuli that you previously linked to your attractiveness, and be as sexually active as you wish. Take the initiative; assume that he is interested until he proves otherwise.

To keep from appearing or feeling desperate, do not let yourself be more completely undressed than he is until his interest is known for certain; undress him yourself if necessary. Otherwise, you risk being fully displayed while he is uninvolved. Make him take a personal risk similar to yours; commit him to the process.

If you have a handicap that is concealed by clothes, then make him touch it before he sees it. If you had a mastectomy, for example, then move his hand under your clothing and rub it gently up and down your ribs before you undress. Represent the touching as sensual and fun; smile confidently if you can manage it. This act is likely to reduce uneasiness greatly; seeing a nonstandard physical attribute may otherwise be a shock and embarrass both of you. Remember that he might not otherwise know how to react tactfully to a newly visible handicap and may hesitate for only that reason; take the lead.

Then, make your first experience as good-feeling for the man as possible, concealing any cramps or other pains from muscular overexertion. Use what you previously studied and learned. You want him to want sex again when you and he next get together. The second time, you can simply tell the truth: the first time was wonderful, but you hurt your hand or got a pain in your back, etc.

Random intermittent positive reinforcement is a strong encouraging force. Casino slot machines pay off irregularly, and people use them eagerly. By making a special effort when you first had sex with the man you seduced, you have started a relationship that supplies exactly that. Sexual experiences of variable intensity will resemble the slot machine; you will have merely rigged the payoff so that the first bet hit the jackpot. Such a payoff scheme will make you seem attractive the first time and will keep him interested, especially if you give him a wonderful experience sometimes but not always. Avoid predictability, not only with sex but also with other aspects of your relationship. Always retain some irregularly delivered positive reinforcement. Fortunately, maintaining irregular positive reinforcement is natural unless a bad habit has been superimposed by a harmful psychological environment. Relax.

If the seduction process is effective enough to surprise you, then hide your surprise. React with happiness and enthusiasm. Pretend that it is natural for a man to be interested in you; and as you gain experience, you will stop needing to pretend. Seem honored that, of people like you, you were his first woman ever.

This process may seem complicated, and it is. But it uses known psychological principles to represent your handicap as an advantage. Many self-appointed experts would pronounce the process impossible. It will not always work; expect it to fail annoyingly often while you learn. But after you do learn it, you will not be bothered by your handicap in a sexual context.

If you want more than sex, then the relationship can grow and develop accordingly. With the sex question permanently solved, and with your clear awareness of your physical abilities and limits, you can guide the relationship very much as if you were able-bodied.

Conclusion

You now know how to take your handicap and transform it to a sex attractant, how and why to approach men, and what to do next. I have tried to show you the entire process, from meeting to sex and beyond. Do you feel better? A happy future awaits you.

Or do you feel worse?

I removed a rationalization from you. You can no longer say "What's the use, it's impossible" about meeting men. Now, you must face your unattached state honestly. That will hurt if a psychological crutch existed that made being alone more comfortable than it is now.

Your new despair, if it exists, is a normal reaction to being alone and wishing for a relationship. The bad feeling is a driving force, trying to prod you into the world so that you can look for someone. The more you resist it, the worse you will feel. Eventually, you will (I hope) start to circulate and meet men. (Did I create a link in you between feeling bad and deciding to circulate? Yes? Good! Such was my need; I wanted to motivate you to try this process so that it can work for you.)

Ideally, this process will become popular; and more and more men will consider handicaps attractive. Cosmetic surgeons will have to stop sculpting their patients and start advising them to take deep dives into shallow pools, hitchhike with drunk drivers, and apprehend armed muggers singlehandedly. Or maybe they will merely tell their patients to engage in activity that is less risky, but that simply reflects the confident energy of well-adjusted people. People who go about their business, and who occasionally get hurt and keep going anyway. People who are busy living, doing, and enjoying.

But isn't that what life is all about?

THE END